Many Voices

E. Nesbit

Contents

THE RETURN	7
FOR DOLLY--WHO DOES NOT LEARN HER LESSONS	10
QUESTIONS	11
THE DAISIES	11
THE TOUCHSTONE	13
THE DECEMBER ROSE	14
THE FIRE	14
SONG	17
A PARTING	18
THE GIFT OF LIFE	19
INCOMPATIBILITIES	20
THE STOLEN GOD--LAZARUS TO DIVES	20
WINTER	23
SEA-SHELLS	24
HOPE	25
THE PRODIGAL'S RETURN	26
THE SKYLARK	27
SATURDAY SONG	28
THE CHAMPION	30
THE GARDEN REFUSED	32
THESE LITTLE ONES	33
THE DESPOT	34
THE MAGIC RING	35
PHILOSOPHY	36
THE WHIRLIGIG OF TIME	37
MAGIC	37
WINDFLOWERS	39
AS IT IS	40
BEFORE WINTER	41
THE VAULT--AFTER SEDGMOOR	42
SURRENDER	43
VALUES	44
IN THE PEOPLE'S PARK	45
WEDDING DAY	46
THE LAST DEFEAT	47
MAY DAY	48
GRETNA GREEN	49
THE ETERNAL	50
THE POINT OF VIEW: I.	51
THE POINT OF VIEW: II.	52
MARY OF MAGDALA	53

THE HOME-COMING	55
AGE TO YOUTH	56
IN AGE	57
WHITE MAGIC	58
FROM THE PORTUGUESE	59
THE NEST	62
THE OLD MAGIC	63
FAITH	64
THE DEATH OF AGNES	65
IN TROUBLE	66
GRATITUDE	67
AT THE LAST	68
FEAR	68
THE DAY OF JUDGMENT	69
A FAREWELL	70
IN HOSPITAL	71
PRAYER IN TIME OF WAR	72
AT PARTING	73
INVOCATION	73
TO HER: IN TIME OF WAR	74
THE FIELDS OF FLANDERS	75
SPRING IN WAR-TIME	76
THE MOTHER'S PRAYER	77
"INASMUCH AS YE DID IT NOT . . . "	79

MANY VOICES

BY
E. Nesbit

THE RETURN

The grass was gray with the moonlit dew,
The stones were white as I came through;
I came down the path by the thirteen yews,
Through the blocks of shade that the moonlight hews.
And when I came to the high lych-gate
I waited awhile where the corpses wait;
Then I came down the road where the moonlight lay
Like the fallen ghost of the light of day.

The bats shrieked high in their zigzag flight,
The owls' spread wings were quiet and white,
The wind and the poplar gave sigh for sigh,
And all about were the rustling shy
Little live creatures that love the night -
Little wild creatures timid and free.
I passed, and they were not afraid of me.

It was over the meadow and down the lane
The way to come to my house again:
Through the wood where the lovers talk,
And the ghosts, they say, get leave to walk.
I wore the clothes that we all must wear,
And no one saw me walking there,

No one saw my pale feet pass
By my garden path to my garden grass.
My garden was hung with the veil of spring -
Plum-tree and pear-tree blossoming;
It lay in the moon's cold sheet of light
In garlands and silence, wondrous and white
As a dead bride decked for her burying.

Then I saw the face of my house
Held close in the arms of the blossomed boughs:
I leaned my face to the window bright
To feel if the heart of my house beat right.
The firelight hung it with fitful gold;
It was warm as the house of the dead is cold.
I saw the settles, the candles tall,
The black-faced presses against the wall,
Polished beechwood and shining brass,
The gleam of china, the glitter of glass,
All the little things that were home to me -
Everything as it used to be.

Then I said, "The fire of life still burns,
And I have returned whence none returns:
I will warm my hands where the fire is lit,
I will warm my heart in the heart of it!"
So I called aloud to the one within:
"Open, open, and let me in!
Let me in to the fire and the light -
It is very cold out here in the night!"
There was never a stir or an answering breath -
Only a silence as deep as death.

Then I beat on the window, and called, and cried.
No one heard me, and none replied.
The golden silence lay warm and deep,
And I wept as the dead, forgotten, weep;
And there was no one to hear or see -
To comfort me, to have pity on me.

But deep in the silence something stirred -
Something that had not seen or heard -
And two drew near to the window-pane,
Kissed in the moonlight and kissed again,
And looked, through my face, to the moon-shroud, spread
Over the garlanded garden bed;
And--"How ghostly the moonlight is!" she said.

Back through the garden, the wood, the lane,
I came to mine own place again.
I wore the garments we all must wear,
And no one saw me walking there.
No one heard my thin feet pass
Through the white of the stones and the gray of the grass,
Along the path where the moonlight hews
Slabs of shadow for thirteen yews.

In the hollow where drifted dreams lie deep
It is good to sleep: it was good to sleep:
But my bed has grown cold with the drip of the dew,
And I cannot sleep as I used to do.

FOR DOLLY--WHO DOES NOT LEARN HER LESSONS

You see the fairies dancing in the fountain,
Laughing, leaping, sparkling with the spray;
You see the gnomes, at work beneath the mountain,
Make gold and silver and diamonds every day;
You see the angels, sliding down the moonbeams,
Bring white dreams like sheaves of lilies fair;
You see the imps, scarce seen against the moonbeams,
Rise from the bonfire's blue and liquid air.

All the enchantment, all the magic there is
Hid in trees and blossoms, to you is plain and true.
Dewdrops in lupin leaves are jewels for the fairies;
Every flower that blows is a miracle for you.
Air, earth, water, fire, spread their splendid wares for you.
Millions of magics beseech your little looks;
Every soul your winged soul meets, loves you and cares for you.
Ah! why must we clip those wings and dim those eyes with books?

Soon, soon enough the magic lights grow dimmer,
Marsh mists arise to cloud the radiant sky,
Dust of hard highways will veil the starry glimmer,
Tired hands will lay the folded magic by.
Storm winds will blow through those enchanted closes,
Fairies be crushed where weed and briar grow strong . . .
Leave her her crown of magic stars and roses,
Leave her her kingdom--she will not keep it long!

QUESTIONS

What do the roses do, mother,
Now that the summer's done?
They lie in the bed that is hung with red
And dream about the sun.

What do the lilies do, mother,
Now that there's no more June?
Each one lies down in her white nightgown
And dreams about the moon.

What can I dream of, mother,
With the moon and the sun away?
Of a rose unborn, of an untried thorn,
And a lily that lives a day!

THE DAISIES

In the great green park with the wooden palings -
The wooden palings so hard to climb,
There are fern and foxglove, primrose and violet,
And green things growing all the time;
And out in the open the daisies grow,
Pretty and proud in their proper places,

Millions of white-frilled daisy faces,
Millions and millions--not one or two.
And they call to the bluebells down in the wood:
"Are you out--are you in? We have been so good
All the school-time winter through,
But now it's playtime,
The gay time, the May time;
We are out and at play. Where are you?"

In the gritty garden inside the railings,
The spiky railings all painted green,
There are neat little beds of geraniums and fuchsia
With never a happy weed between.
There's a neat little grass plot, bald in places,
And very dusty to touch;
A respectable man comes once a week
To keep the garden weeded and swept,
To keep it as we don't want it kept.
He cuts the grass with his mowing-machine,
And we think he cuts it too much.
But even on the lawn, all dry and gritty,
The daisies play about.
They are so brave as well as so pretty,
You cannot keep them out.
I love them, I want to let them grow,
But that respectable man says no.
He cuts off their heads with his mowing-machine
Like the French Revolution guillotine.
He sweeps up the poor little pretty faces,
The dear little white-frilled daisy faces;
Says things must be kept in their proper places
He has no frill round his ugly face -
I wish I could find his proper place!

THE TOUCHSTONE

There was a garden, very strange and fair
With all the roses summer never brings.
The snowy blossom of immortal Springs
Lighted its boughs, and I, even I, was there.
There were new heavens, and the earth was new,
And still I told my heart the dream was true.

But when the sun stood still, and Time went out
Like a blown candle--when she came to me
Under the bride-veil of the blossomed tree,
Chill through the garden blew the winds of doubt,
And when, with starry eyes, and lips too near,
She leaned to me, my heart knew what to fear.

"It is no dream," she said. "What dream had stayed
So long? It is the blessed isle that lies
Between the tides of twin eternities.
It is our island; do not be afraid!"
Then, then at last my heart was well deceived;
I hid my eyes; I trembled and believed.

Her real presence sanctified my faith,
Her very voice my restless fears beguiled,
And it was Life that clasped me when she smiled,
But when she said "I love you!" it was Death.
That, that at least could neither be nor seem -
Oh, then, indeed, I knew it was a dream!

THE DECEMBER ROSE

Here's a rose that blows for Chloe,
Fair as ever a rose in June was,
Now the garden's silent, snowy,
Where the burning summer noon was.

In your garden's summer glory
One poor corner, shelved and shady,
Told no rosy, radiant story,
Grew no rose to grace its lady.

What shuts sun out shuts out snow too;
From his nook your secret lover
Shows what slighted roses grow to
When the rose you chose is over.

THE FIRE

I was picking raspberries, my head was in the canes,
And he came behind and kissed me, and I smacked him for his pains.
Says he, "You take it easy! That ain't the way to do!
I love you hot as fire, my girl, and you know you know it too.
So won't you name the day?"
But I said, "That I will not."

And I pushed him away,
Out among the raspberries all on a summer day.
And I says, "You ask in winter, if your love's so hot,
For it's summer now, and sunny, and my hands is full," says I,
"With the fair by and by,
And the village dance and all;
And the turkey poults is small,
And so's the ducks and chicks,
And the hay not yet in ricks,
And the flower-show'll be presently and hop-picking's to come,
And the fruiting and the harvest home,
And my new white gown to make, and the jam all to be done.
Can't you leave a girl alone?
Your love's too hot for me!
Can't you leave a girl be
Till the evenings do draw in,
Till the leaves be getting thin,
Till the fires be lighted early, and the curtains drawed for tea?
That's the time to do your courting, if you come a-courting me!"

* * *

And he took it as I said it, an' not as it was meant.
And he went.

* * *

The hay was stacked, the fruit was picked, the hops were dry and brown,
And everything was garnered, and the year turned upside down,
And the winter it come on, and the fires were early lit,
And he'd never come anigh again, and all my life was sick.
And I was cold alone, with nought to do but sit

With my hands in my black lap, and hear the clock tick.
For father, he lay dead
With the candles at his head,
And his coffin was that black I could see it through the wall;
And I'd sent them all away,
Though they'd offered for to stay.
I wanted to be cold alone, and learn to bear it all.
Then I heard him. I'd a-known it for his footstep just as plain
If he'd brought his regiment with him up the rutty frozen lane.
And I hadn't drawn the curtains, and I see him through the pane;
And I jumped up in my blacks and I threw the door back wide.
Says I, "You come inside;
For it's cold outside for you,
And it's cold here too;
And I haven't no more pride -
It's too cold for that," I cried.

* * *

Then I saw in his face
The fear of death, and desire.
And oh, I took and kissed him again and again,
And I clipped him close and all,
In the winter, in the dusk, in the quiet house-place,
With the coffin lying black and full the other side the wall;
And "YOU warm my heart," I told him, "if there's any fire in men!"
And he got his two arms round me, and I felt the fire then.
And I warmed my heart at the fire.

SONG

Now the Spring is waking,
Very shy as yet,
Busy mending, making
Grass and violet.
Frowsy Winter's over:
See the budding lane!
Go and meet your lover:
Spring is here again!

Every day is longer
Than the day before;
Lambs are whiter, stronger,
Birds sing more and more;
Woods are less than shady,
Griefs are more than vain -
Go and kiss your lady:
Spring is here again!

A PARTING

So good-bye!
This is where we end it, you and I.
Life's to live, you know, and death's to die;
So good-bye!

I was yours
For the love in life that loves while life endures,
For the earth-path that the Heaven-flight ensures
I was yours.

You were mine
For the moment that a garland takes to twine,
For the human hour that sorcery shews divine
You were mine.

All is over.
You and I no more are love and lover;
Nought's to seek now, gain, attain, discover.
All is over.

THE GIFT OF LIFE

Life is a night all dark and wild,
Yet still stars shine:
This moment is a star, my child -
Your star and mine.

Life is a desert dry and drear,
Undewed, unblest;
This hour is an oasis, dear;
Here let us rest.

Life is a sea of windy spray,
Cold, fierce and free:
An isle enchanted is to-day
For you and me.

Forget night, sea, and desert: take
The gift supreme,
And, of life's brief relenting, make
A deathless dream.

INCOMPATIBILITIES

If you loved me I could trust you to your fancy's furthest bound
While the sun shone and the wind blew, and the world went round,
To the utmost of the meshes of the devil's strongest net . . .
If you loved me, if you loved me--but you do not love me yet!

I love you--and I cannot trust you further than the door!
But winds and worlds and seasons change, and you will love me more
And more--until I trust you, dear, as women do trust men -
I shall trust you, I shall trust you, but I shall not love you
then!

THE STOLEN GOD--LAZARUS TO DIVES

We do not clamour for vengeance,
We do not whine for fear;
We have cried in the outer darkness
Where was no man to hear.
We cried to man and he heard not;
Yet we thought God heard us pray;
But our God, who loved and was sorry -
Our God is taken away.

Ours were the stream and the pasture,

Forest and fen were ours;
Ours were the wild wood-creatures,
The wild sweet berries and flowers.
You have taken our heirlooms from us,
And hardly you let us save
Enough of our woods for a cradle,
Enough of our earth for a grave.

You took the wood and the cornland,
Where still we tilled and felled;
You took the mine and quarry,
And all you took you held.
The limbs of our weanling children
You crushed in your mills of power;
And you made our bearing women toil
To the very bearing hour.

You have taken our clean quick longings,
Our joy in lover and wife,
Our hope of the sunset quiet
At the evening end of life;
You have taken the land that bore us,
Its soil and stone and sod;
You have taken our faith in each other -
And now you have taken our God.

When our God came down from Heaven
He came among men, a Man,
Eating and drinking and working
As common people can;
And the common people received Him
While the rich men turned away.
But what have we to do with a God

To whom the rich men pray?

He hangs, a dead God, on your altars,
Who lived a Man among men,
You have taken away our Lord
And we cannot find Him again.
You have not left us a handful
Of even the earth He trod . . .
You have made Him a rich man's idol
Who came as a poor man's God.

He promised the poor His heaven,
He loved and lived with the poor;
He said that the rich man's shadow
Should never darken His door:
But bishops and priests lie softly,
Drink full and are fully fed
In the Name of the Lord, who had not
Where to lay His head.

This is the God you have stolen,
As you steal all else--in His name.
You have taken the ease and the honour,
Left us the toil and the shame.
You have chosen the seat of Dives,
We lie where Lazarus lay;
But, by God, we will not yield you our God,
You shall not take Him away.

All else we had you have taken;
All else, but not this, not this.
The God of Heaven is ours, is ours,
And the poor are His, are His.

Is He ours? Is He yours? Give answer!
For both He cannot be.
And if He is ours--O you rich men,
Then whose, in God's name, are ye?

WINTER

Hold your hands to the blaze;
Winter is here
With the short cold days,
Bleak, keen and drear.
Was there ever a day
With hawthorn along the way
Where you wandered in mild mid-May
With your dear?

That was when you were young
And the world was gold;
Now all the songs are sung,
The tales all told.
You shiver now by the fire
Where the last red sparks expire;
Dead are delight and desire:
You are old.

SEA-SHELLS

I gathered shells upon the sand,
Each shell a little perfect thing,
So frail, yet potent to withstand
The mountain-waves' wild buffeting.
Through storms no ship could dare to brave
The little shells float lightly, save
All that they might have lost of fine
Shape and soft colour crystalline.

Yet I amid the world's wild surge
Doubt if my soul can face the strife,
The waves of circumstance that urge
That slight ship on the rocks of life.
O soul, be brave, for He who saves
The frail shell in the giant waves,
Will bring thy puny bark to land
Safe in the hollow of His hand.

HOPE

O thrush, is it true?
Your song tells
Of a world born anew,
Of fields gold with buttercups, woodlands all blue
With hyacinth bells;
Of primroses deep
In the moss of the lane,
Of a Princess asleep
And dear magic to do.
Will the sun wake the princess? O thrush, is it true?
Will Spring come again?

Will Spring come again?
Now at last
With soft shine and rain
Will the violet be sweet where the dead leaves have lain?
Will Winter be past?
In the brown of the copse
Will white wind-flowers star through
Where the last oak-leaf drops?
Will the daisies come too,
And the may and the lilac? Will Spring come again?
O thrush, is it true?

THE PRODIGAL'S RETURN

I reach my hand to thee!
Stoop; take my hand in thine;
Lead me where I would be,
Father divine.
I do not even know
The way I want to go,
The way that leads to rest:
But, Thou who knowest me,
Lead where I cannot see,
Thou knowest best.

Toys, worthless, yet desired,
Drew me afar to roam.
Father, I am so tired;
I am come home.
The love I held so cheap
I see, so dear, so deep,
So almost understood.
Life is so cold and wild,
I am thy little child -
I WILL be good.

THE SKYLARK

". . . a dripping shower of notes from the softening blue. It is the skylark come."--Robert A Field, in the New Age.

"It is the skylark come." For shame!
Robert-a-Cockney is thy name:
Robert-a-Field would surely know
That skylarks, bless them, never go!

* * *

Love of my life, bear witness here
How we have heard them all the year;
How to the skylark's song are set
The days we never can forget.
At Rustington, do you remember?
We heard the skylarks in December;
In January above the snow
They sang to us by Hurstmonceux
Once in the keenest airs of March
We heard them near the Marble Arch;
Their April song thrilled Tonbridge air;
May found them singing everywhere;
And oh, in Sheppey, how their tune
Rhymed with the bean-flower scent in June.
One unforgotten day at Rye
They sang a love-song in July;
In August, hard by Lewes town,
They sang of joy 'twixt sky and down;

And in September's golden spell
We heard them singing on Scaw Fell.
October's leaves were brown and sere,
But skylarks sang by Teston Weir;
And in November, at Mount's Bay,
They sang upon our wedding day!

* * *

Mr.-a-Field, go forth, go forth,
Go east and west and south and north;
You'll always find the furze in flower,
Find every hour the lovers' hour,
And, by my faith in love and rhyme,
The skylark singing all the time!

SATURDAY SONG

They talk about gardens of roses,
And moonlight over the sea,
And mountains and snow
And sunsetty glow,
But I know what is best for me.
The prettiest sight I know,
Worth all your roses and snow,
Is the blaze of light on a Saturday night,
When the barrows are set in a row.

I've heard of bazaars in India

All glitter and spices and smells,
But they don't compare
With the naphtha flare
And the herrings the coster sells;
And the oranges piled like gold,
The cucumbers lean and cold,
And the red and white block-trimmings
And the strawberries fresh and ripe,
And the peas and beans,
And the sprouts and greens,
And the 'taters and trotters and tripe.

And the shops where they sell the chairs,
The mangles and tables and bedding,
And the lovers go by in pairs,
And look--and think of the wedding.
And your girl has her arm in yours,
And you whisper and make her blush.
Oh! the snap in her eyes--and her smiles and her sighs
As she fancies the purple plush!

And you haven't a penny to spend,
But you dream that you've pounds and pounds;
And arm in arm with your only friend
You make your Saturday rounds:
And you see the cradle bright
With ribbon--lace--pink and white;
And she stops her laugh
And you drop your chaff
In the light of the Saturday night.
And the world is new
For her and you -
A little bit of all-right.

THE CHAMPION

Young and a conqueror, once on a day,
Wild white Winter rode out this way;
With his sword of ice and his banner of snow
Vanquished the Summer and laid her low.

Winter was young then, young and strong;
Now he is old, he has reigned too long.
He shall be routed, he shall be slain;
Summer shall come to her own again!

See the champion of Summer wake
Little armies in field and brake:
"Cruel and cold has King Winter been;
Fight for the Summer, fight for the Queen!"

First the aconite dots the mould
With little round cannon-balls of gold;
Then, to help in the winter's rout,
Regiments of crocuses march out.

See the swords of the flag-leaves shine;
See the shield of the celandine,
And daffodil lances green and keen,
To fight for the Summer, fight for the Queen.

Silver triumphant the snowdrop swings
Banners that mock at defeated kings;
And wherever the green of the new grass peers,
See the array of victorious spears.
Daffodil trumpets soon shall sound

Over the garden's battle-ground,
And lovely ladies crowd out to see
The long procession of victory.

Little daisies with snowy frills,
Courtly tulips and sweet jonquils,
Primrose and cowslip, friends well met
With white wood-sorrel and violet.

Hundreds of milkmaids by field and fold;
Thousands of buttercups licked with gold;
Budding hedges and woods and trees -
Spring brings freedom and life to these.

Then the triumphant Spring shall ride
Over the happy countryside;
Deep in the woods the birds shall sing:
"The King is dead--long live the King!"

But Spring is no king, but a faithful knight;
He will ride on through the meadows bright
Till at Summer's feet he shall light him down
And lay at her feet the royal crown.

She will lean down where the roses twine
Between the may-trees' silver shine,
And look in the eyes of the dying knight
Who led his army and won her fight.

She will stoop to his lips and say,
"Oh, live, O love! O my true love, stay!"
While he smiles and sighs her arms between
And dies for the Summer, dies for the Queen.

THE GARDEN REFUSED

There is a garden made for our delight,
Where all the dreams we dare not dream come true.
I know it, but I do not know the way.
We slip and tumble in the doubtful night,
Where everything is difficult and new,
And clouds our breath has made obscure the day.

The blank unhappy towns, where sick men strive,
Still doing work that yet is never done;
The hymns to Gold that drown their desperate voice;
The weeds that grow where once corn stood alive,
The black injustice that puts out the sun:
These are our portion, since they are our choice.

Yet there the garden blows with rose on rose,
The sunny, shadow-dappled lawns are there;
There the immortal lilies, heavenly sweet.
O roses, that for us shall not unclose!
O lilies, that we shall not pluck or wear!
O dewy lawns untrodden by our feet!

THESE LITTLE ONES

"What of the garden I gave?"
God said to me;
"Hast thou been diligent to foster and save
The life of flower and tree?
How have the roses thriven,
The lilies I have given,
The pretty scented miracles that Spring
And Summer come to bring?

"My garden is fair and dear,"
I said to God;
"From thorns and nettles I have kept it clear.
Green-trimmed its sod.
The rose is red and bright,
The lily a live delight;
I have not lost a flower of all the flowers
That blessed my hours."

"What of the child I gave?"
God said to me;
"The little, little one I died to save
And gave in trust to thee?
How have the flowers grown
That in its soul were sown,
The lovely living miracles of youth
And hope and joy and truth?"

"The child's face is all white,"
I said to God;
"It cries for cold and hunger in the night:
Its little feet have trod
The pavement muddy and cold.
It has no flowers to hold,
And in its soul the flowers you set are dead."
"Thou fool!" God said.

THE DESPOT

The garden mould was damp and chill;
Winter had had his brutal will
Since over all the year's content
His devastating legions went.

The Spring's bright banners came: there woke
Millions of little growing folk
Who thrilled to know the winter done,
Gave thanks, and strove towards the sun.

Not so the elect; reserved, and slow
To trust a stranger-sun and grow,
They hesitated, cowered and hid,
Waiting to see what others did.

Yet even they, a little, grew,
Put out prim leaves to day and dew,
And lifted level formal heads

In their appointed garden beds.

The gardener came: he coldly loved
The flowers that lived as he approved,
That duly, decorously grew
As he, the despot, meant them to.

He saw the wildlings flower more brave
And bright than any cultured slave;
Yet, since he had not set them there,
He hated them for being fair.

So he uprooted, one by one,
The free things that had loved the sun,
The happy, eager, fruitful seeds
Who had not known that they were weeds.

THE MAGIC RING

Your touch on my hand is fire,
Your lips on my lips are flowers.
My darling, my one desire,
Dear crown of my days and hours.
Dear crown of each hour and day
Since ever my life began.
Ah! leave me--ah! go away -
We two are woman and man.

To lie in your arms and see
The stars melt into the sun;
Till there is no you and me,
Since you and I are one.
To loose my soul to your breath,
To bare my heart to your life -
It is death, it is death, it is death!
I am not your wife.

The hours will come and will go,
But never again such an hour
When the tides immortal flow
And life is a flood, a flower . . .
Wait for the ring; it is strong,
It has a magic of might
To make all that was splendid and wrong
Sordid and right.

PHILOSOPHY

The sulky sage scarce condescends to see
This pretty world of sun and grass and leaves;
To him 'tis all illusion--only he
Is real amid the visions he perceives.

No sage am I, and yet, by Love's decree,
To me the world's a masque of shadows too,
And I a shadow also--since to me
The only real thing in life is--you.

THE WHIRLIGIG OF TIME

Before your feet,
My love, my sweet,
Behold! your slave bows down;
And in his hands
From other lands
Brings you another crown.

For in far climes,
In bygone times,
Myself was royal too:
Oh, I have been
A king, my queen,
Who am a slave for you!

MAGIC

What was the spell she wove for me?
Life was a common useful thing,
An eligible building site
To hold a house to shelter me.
There were no woodlands whispering;
No unimagined dreams at night
About that house had folded wing,

Disordering my life for me.

I was so safe until she came
With starry secrets in her eyes,
And on her lips the word of power.
- Like to the moon of May she came,
That makes men mad who were born wise -
Within her hand the only flower
Man ever plucked from Paradise;
So to my half-built house she came.

She turned my useful plot of land
Into a garden wild and fair,
Where stars in garlands hung like flowers:
A moonlit, lonely, lovely land.
Dim groves and glimmering fountains there
Embraced a secret bower of bowers,
And in its rose-ringed heart we were
Alone in that enchanted land.

What was the spell I wove for her,
Her mad dear magic to undo?
The red rose dies, the white rose dies,
The garden spits me forth with her
On the old suburban road I knew.
My house is gone, and by my side
A stranger stands with angry eyes
And lips that swear I ruined her.

WINDFLOWERS

When I was little and good
I walked in the dappled wood
Where light white windflowers grew,
And hyacinths heavy and blue.

The windflowers fluttered light,
Like butterflies white and bright;
The bluebells tremulous stood
Deep in the heart of the wood.

I gathered the white and the blue,
The wild wet woodland through,
With hands too silly and small
To clasp and carry them all.

Some dropped from my hands and died
By the home-road's grassy side;
And those that my fond hands pressed
Died even before the rest.

AS IT IS

If you and I
Had wings to fly -
Great wings like seagulls' wings -
How would we soar
Above the roar
Of loud unneeded things!

We two would rise
Through changing skies
To blue unclouded space,
And undismayed
And unafraid
Meet the sun face to face.

But wings we know not;
The feathers grow not
To carry us so high;
And low in the gloom
Of a little room
We weep and say good-bye.

BEFORE WINTER

The wind is crying in the night,
Like a lost child;
The waves break wonderful and white
And wild.
The drenched sea-poppies swoon along
The drenched sea-wall,
And there's an end of summer and of song -
An end of all.

The fingers of the tortured boughs
Gripped by the blast
Clutch at the windows of your house
Closed fast.
And the lost child of love, despair,
Cries in the night,
Remembering how once those windows were
Open and bright.

THE VAULT--AFTER SEDGMOOR

You need not call at the Inn;
I have ordered my bed:
Fair linen sheets therein
And a tester of lead.
No musty fusty scents
Such as inn chambers keep,
But tapestried with content
And hung with sleep.

My Inn door bears no bar
Set up against fear.
The guests have journeyed far,
They are glad to be here.
Where the damp arch curves up grey,
Long, long shall we lie;
Good King's men all are they,
A King's man I.

Old Giles, in his stone asleep,
Fought at Poictiers.
Piers Ralph and Roger keep
The spoil of their fighting years.
I shall lie with my folk at last
In a quiet bed;
I shall dream of the sword held fast
In a round-capped head.

Good tale of men all told
My Inn affords;
And their hands peace shall hold
That once held swords.
And we who rode and ran
On many a loyal quest
Shall find the goal of man -
A bed, and rest.

We shall not stand to the toast
Of Love or King;
We be all too tired to boast
About anything.
We be dumb that did jest and sing;
We rest who laboured and warred . . .
Shout once, shout once for the King.
Shout once for the sword!

SURRENDER

Oh, the nights were dark and cold,
When my love was gone.
And life was hard to hold
When my love was gone.
I was wise, I never gave
What they teach a girl to save,
But I wished myself his slave
When my love was gone.

I was all alone at night
When my love came home.
Oh, what thought of wrong or right
When my love came home?
I flung the door back wide
And I pulled my love inside;
There was no more shame or pride
When my love came home.

VALUES

Did you deceive me? Did I trust
A heart of fire to a heart of dust?
What matter? Since once the world was fair,
And you gave me the rose of the world to wear.

That was the time to live for! Flowers,
Sunshine and starshine and magic hours,
Summer about me, Heaven above,
And all seemed immortal, even Love.

Well, the mortal rose of your love was worth
The pains of death and the pains of birth;
And the thorns may be sharper than death--who knows? -
That crowd round the stem of a deathless rose.

IN THE PEOPLE'S PARK

Many's the time I've found your face
Fresh as a bunch of flowers in May,
Waiting for me at our own old place
At the end of the working day.
Many's the time I've held your hand
On the shady seat in the People's Park,
And blessed the blaring row of the band
And kissed you there in the dark.

Many's the time you promised true,
Swore it with kisses, swore it with tears:
"I'll marry no one without it's you -
If we have to wait for years."
And now it's another chap in the Park
That holds your hand like I used to do;
And I kiss another girl in the dark,
And try to fancy it's you!

WEDDING DAY

The enchanted hour,
The magic bower,
Where, crowned with roses,
Love love discloses.

"Kiss me, my lover;
Doubting is over,
Over is waiting;
Love lights our mating!"

"But roses wither,
Chill winds blow hither,
One thing all say, dear,
Love lives a day, dear!"

"Heed those old stories?
New glowing glories
Blot out those lies, love!
Look in my eyes, love!

"Ah, but the world knows -
Naught of the true rose;
Back the world slips, love!
Give me your lips, love!

"Even were their lies true,
Yet were you wise to
Swear, at Love's portal,
The god's immortal."

THE LAST DEFEAT

Across the field of day
In sudden blazon lay
The pallid bar of gold
Borne on the shield of day.
Night had endured so long,
And now the Day grew strong
With lance of light to hold
The Night at bay.

So on my life's dull night
The splendour of your light
Traversed the dusky shield
And shone forth golden bright.
Your colours I have worn
Through all the fight forlorn,
And these, with life, I yield,
To-night, to Night.

MAY DAY

Will you go a-maying, a-maying, a-maying,
Come and be my Queen of May and pluck the may with me?
The fields are full of daisy buds and new lambs playing,
The bird is on the nest, dear, the blossom's on the tree."

"If I go with you, if I go a-maying,
To be your Queen and wear my crown this May-day bright,
Hand in hand straying, it must be only playing,
And playtime ends at sunset, and then good-night.

"For I have heard of maidens who laughed and went a-maying,
Went out queens and lost their crowns and came back slaves.
I will be no young man's slave, submitting and obeying,
Bearing chains as those did, even to their graves."

"If you come a-maying, a-straying, a-playing,
We will pluck the little flowers, enough for you and me;
And when the day dies, end our one day's playing,
Give a kiss and take a kiss and go home free."

GRETNA GREEN

Last night when I kissed you,
My soul caught alight;
And oh! how I missed you
The rest of the night -
Till Love in derision
Smote sleep with his wings,
And gave me in vision
Impossible things.

A night that was clouded,
Long windows asleep;
Dark avenues crowded
With secrets to keep.
A terrace, a lover,
A foot on the stair;
The waiting was over,
The lady was there.

What a flight, what a night!
The hoofs splashed and pounded.
Dark fainted in light
And the first bird-notes sounded.
You slept on my shoulder,
Shy night hid your face;
But dawn, bolder, colder,
Beheld our embrace.

Your lips of vermilion,
Your ravishing shape,
The flogging postillion,
The village agape,
The rattle and thunder
Of postchaise a-speed . . .
My woman, my wonder,
My ultimate need!

We two matched for mating
Came, handclasped, at last,
Where the blacksmith was waiting
To fetter us fast . . .
At the touch of the fetter
The dream snapped and fell -
And I woke to your letter
That bade me farewell.

THE ETERNAL

Your dear desired grace,
Your hands, your lips of red,
The wonder of your perfect face
Will fade, like sweet rose-petals shed,
When you are dead.

Your beautiful hair
Dust in the dust will lie -
But not the light I worship there,

The gold the sunshine crowns you by -
This will not die.

Your beautiful eyes
Will be closed up with clay;
But all the magic they comprise,
The hopes, the dreams, the ecstasies
Pass not away.

All I desire and see
Will be a carrion thing;
But all that you have been to me
Is, and can never cease to be.
O Grave! where is thy victory?
Where, Death, thy sting?

THE POINT OF VIEW: I.

I

There was never winter, summer only: roses,
Pink and white and red,
Shining down the warm rich garden closes;
Quiet trees and lawns of dappled shadow,
Silver lilies, whisper of mignonette,
Cloth-of-gold of buttercups outspread;
Good gold sun that kissed me when we met,
Shadows of floating clouds on sunny meadow.
In the hay-field, scented, grey,

Loving life and love, I lay;
By fresh airs blown, drifted into sleep;
Slept and dreamed there. Winter was the dream.

II

Summer never was, was always winter only;
Cold and ice and frost
Only, driven by the ice-wind, lonely,
In a world of strangers, in the welter
Of the puddles and the spiteful wind and sleet,
Blinded by the spitting hailstones, lost
In a bitter unfamiliar street,
I found a doorway, crouched there for just shelter,
Crouched and fought in vain for breath,
Cursed the cold and wished for death;
Crouched there, gathered somehow warmth to sleep;
Slept and dreamed there. Summer was the dream.

THE POINT OF VIEW: II.

I

In the wood of lost causes, the valley of tears,
Old hopes, like dead leaves, choke the difficult way;
Dark pinions fold dank round the soul, and it hears:
"It is night, it is night, it has never been day;
Thou hast dreamed of the day, of the rose of delight;
It was always dead leaves and the heart of the night.

Drink deep then, and rest, O thou foolish wayfarer,
For night, like a chalice, holds sleep in her hands."

II

Then you drain the dark cup, and, half-drugged as you lie
In the arms of despair that is masked as delight,
You thrill to the rush of white wings, and you hear:
"It is day, it is day, it has never been night!
Thou hast dreamed of the night and the wood of lost leaves;
It was always noon, June, and red roses in sheaves,
Unlock the blind lids, and behold the light-bearer
Who holds, like a monstrance, the sun in his hands."

MARY OF MAGDALA

Mary of Magdala came to bed;
There were no soft curtains round her head;
She had no mother to hold of worth
The little baby she brought to birth.

Mary of Magdala groaned and prayed:
"O God, I am very much afraid;
For out of my body, by sin defiled,
Thou biddest me make a little child.

"O God, I have turned my face from Thee
To that which the angels may not see;
How can I make, from my deep disgrace,

A child whose angel shall see Thy face?

"O God, I have sinned, and I know well
That the pains I bear are the pains of hell;
But the thought of the child that sin has given
Is like the thought of the airs of Heaven."

Mary of Magdala held her breath
In the clutch of pain like the pains of Death,
And through her heart, like the mortal knife,
Went the pang of joy and the pang of life.

"We two are two alone," said she,
"And we are two who should be three;
Now who will clothe my baby fair
In the little garments that babies wear?"

There came two angels with quiet wings
And hands that were full of baby things;
And the new-born child was bathed and dressed
And laid again on his mother's breast.

"Now who will sign on his brow the mark
To keep him safe from the Powers of the Dark?
Who will my baby's sponsor be?"
"I, the Lord God, who died for thee."

"Now who will comfort him if he cry;
And who will suckle him by and bye?
For my hands are cold and my breasts are dry,
And I think that my time has come to die."

"I will dandle thy son as a mother may;
And his lips shall lie where my own Son's lay.
Come, dear little one, come to me;
The Mother of God shall suckle thee."

Mary of Magdala laughed and sighed;
"I never deserved a child," she cried.
"Dear God, I am ready to go to hell,
Since with my little one all is well."

Then the Son of Mary did o'er her lean.
"Poor mother, thy tears have washed thee clean.
Thy last poor pains, they will soon be done,
And My Mother shall give thee back thy son."

Frozen grass for a bearing bed,
A halo of frost round a woman's head,
And pious folks who looked and said:
"A drab and her brat that are better dead."

THE HOME-COMING

This was our house. To this we came
Lighted by love with torch aflame,
And in this chamber, door locked fast,
I held you to my heart at last.

This was our house. In this we knew
The worst that Time and Fate can do.

You left the room bare, wide the door;
You did not love me any more.

Where once the kind warm curtain hung
The spider's ghostly cloth is flung;
The beetle and the woodlouse creep
Where once I loved your lovely sleep.

Yet so the vanished spell endures,
That this, our house, still, still is yours.
Here, spite of all these years apart,
I still can hold you to my heart!

AGE TO YOUTH

Sunrise is in your eyes, and in your heart
The hope and bright desire of morn and May.
My eyes are full of shadow, and my part
Of life is yesterday.

Yet lend my hand your hand, and let us sit
And see your life unfolding like a scroll,
Rich with illuminated blazon, fit
For your arm-bearing soul.

My soul bears arms too, but the scroll's rolled tight,
Yet the one strip of faded brightness shown
Proclaims that when 'twas splendid in the light
Its blazon matched your own.

IN AGE

The wine of life was rough and new,
But sweet beyond belief,
And wrong was false, and right was true -
The rose was in the leaf.

In that good sunlight well we knew
The hues of wrong and right;
We slept among the roses through
The long enchanted night.

Now to our eyes, made dim with years,
Right intertwines with wrong.
How can we hear, with these tired ears,
The old, the magic song?

But this we know--wine once was red,
Roses were red and dear;
Once in our ears the truths were said
That now the young men hear!

WHITE MAGIC

This is the room to which she came,
And Spring itself came with her;
She stirred the fire of life to flame,
She called all music hither.
Her glance upon the lean white walls
Hung them with cloth of splendour,
And still the rose she dropped recalls
The graces that attend her.

The same poor room, so dull and bare
Before, in consecration,
She breathed upon its common air
The true transfiguration . . .?
This room the same to which she came
For one immortal minute? –
How can it ever be the same
Since she has once been in it!

FROM THE PORTUGUESE

I

When I lived in the village of youth
There were lilies in all the orchards,
Flowers in the orange-gardens
For brides to wear in their hair.
It was always sunshine and summer,
Roses at every lattice,
Dreams in the eyes of maidens,
Love in the eyes of men.

When I lived in the village of youth
The doors, all the doors, stood open;
We went in and out of them laughing,
Laughing and calling each other
To shew each other our fairings,
The new shawl, the new comb, the new fan,
The new rose, the new lover.

Now I live in the town of age
Where are no orchards, no gardens.
Here, too, all the doors stand open,
But no one goes in or goes out.
We sit alone by the hearthstone
Where memories lie like ashes
Upon a hearth that is cold;

And they from the village of youth
Run by our doorsteps laughing,
Calling, to shew each other
The new shawl, the new comb, the new fan,
The new rose, the new lover.

Once we had all these things -
We kept them from the old people,
And now the young people have them
And will not shew them to us -
To us who are old and have nothing
But the white, still, heaped-up ashes
On the hearth where the fire went out
A very long time ago.

II

I had a mistress; I loved her.
She left me with memories bitter,
Corroding, eating my heart
As the acid eats into the steel
Etching the portrait triumphant.
Intolerable, indelible,
Never to be effaced.

A wife was mine to my heart,
Beautiful flower of my garden,
Lily I worshipped by day,
Scented rose of my nights.
Now the night wind sighing
Blows white rose petals only
Over the bed where she sleeps
Dreamless alone.

I had a son; I loved him.
Mother of God, bear witness
How all my manhood loved him
As thy womanhood loved thy Son!
When he was grown to his manhood
He crucified my heart,
And even as it hung bleeding
He laughed with his bold companions,
Mocked and turned away
With laughter into the night.

Those three I loved and lost;
But there was one who loved me
With all the fire of her heart.
Mine was the sacred altar
Where she burnt her life for my worship.
She was my slave, my servant;
Mine all she had, all she was,
All she could suffer, could be.
That was the love of my life,
I did not say, "She loves me";
I was so used to her love
I never asked its name,
Till, feeling the wind blow cold
Where all the doors were left open,
And seeing a fireless hearth
And the garden deserted and weed-grown
That once was full of flowers for me,
I said, "What has changed? What is it
That has made all the clocks stop?"
Thus I asked and they answered:
"It is thy mother who is dead."

And now I am alone.
My son, too, some day will stand
Here, where I stand and weep.
He too will weep, knowing too late
The love that wrapped round his life.
Dear God spare him this:
Let him never know how I loved him,
For he was always weak.
He could not endure as I can.
Mother, my dear, ask God
To grant me this, for my son!

THE NEST

That was the skylark we heard
Singing so high,
The little quivering bird
We saw, and the sky.
The earth was drenched with sun,
The sky was drenched with song;
We lay in the grass and listened,
Long and long and long.

I said, "What a spell it is
Has made her rise
To pour out her world of bliss
In that world of skies!"
You said, "What a spell must pass
Between sky and plain,

Since she finds in this world of grass
Her nest again!"

THE OLD MAGIC

Gray is the sea, and the skies are gray;
They are ghosts of our blue, bright yesterday;
And gray are the breasts of the gulls that scream
Like tortured souls in an evil dream.

There is white on the wings of the sea and sky,
And white are the gulls' wings wheeling by,
And white, like snow, is the pall that lies
Where love weeps over his memories.

For the dead is dead, and its shroud is wrought
Of good unfound and of wrong unsought;
Yet from God's good magic there ever springs
The resurrection of holy things.

See--the gold and blue of our yesterday
In the eyes and the hair of a child at play;
And the spell of joy that our youth beguiled
Is woven anew in the laugh of the child.

FAITH

A wall
Gray and tall,
And a sky of gray,
And a twilight cold;
And that is all
That my eyes behold.
But I know that unseen,
Beyond the wall,
On a lawn of green
White blossoms fall
In the waning light;
And beyond the lawn
Curtains are drawn
From windows bright.
And within she moves with her gracious hands
And the heart that loves and that understands,
Waiting to succour poor souls in need,
And to bind with her blessing the hearts that bleed.

I know it all, though I cannot see;
But the tired-out tramp,
Dirty and ill,
In the evening's damp,
In the Spring's clean chill,
Knows not that there
Is the heart to care
For such as I and for such as he.
He slouches along, and sees alone
The gray of the sky and the gray of the stone.

Lord, when my eyes see nothing but grey
In all Thy world that is now so green,
I will bethink me of this spring day
And the house of welcome, known yet unseen;
The wall that conceals
And the faith that reveals.

THE DEATH OF AGNES

Now that the sunlight dies in my eyes,
And the moonlight grows in my hair,
I who was never very wise,
Never was very fair,
Virgin and martyr all my life,
What has life left to give
Me--who was never mother nor wife,
Never got leave to live?

Nothing of life could I clasp or claim,
Nothing could steal or save.
So when you come to carve my name,
Give me life in my grave.
To keep me warm when I sleep alone
A lie is little to give;
Call me "Magdalen" on my stone,
Though I died and did not live.

IN TROUBLE

It's all for nothing: I've lost him now.
I suppose it had to be;
But oh, I never thought it of him,
Nor he never thought it of me.
And all for a kiss on your evening out,
And a field where the grass was down . . .
And he 'as gone to God-knows-where,
And I may go on the town.

The worst of all was the thing he said
The night that he went away;
He said he'd 'a married me right enough
If I hadn't 'a been so gay.
Me--gay! When I'd cried, and I'd asked him not,
But he said he loved me so;
An' whatever he wanted seemed right to me . . .
An' how was a girl to know?

Well, the river is deep, and drowned folk sleep sound,
An' it might be the best to do;
But when he made me a light-o'-love
He made me a mother too.
I've had enough sin to last my time,
If 'twas sin as I got it by,
But it ain't no sin to stand by his kid
And work for it till I die.

But oh! the long days and the death-long nights
When I feel it move and turn,
And cry alone in my single bed
And count what a girl can earn
To buy the baby the bits of things
HE ought to ha' bought, by rights;
And wonder whether he thinks of Us . . .
And if he sleeps sound o' nights.

GRATITUDE

I found a starving cat in the street:
It cried for food and a place by the fire.
I carried it home, and I strove to meet
The claims of its desire.

And since its desire was a little fish,
A little hay and a little milk,
I gave it cream in a silver dish
And a basket lined with silk.

And when we came to the grateful pause
When it should have fawned on the hand that fed,
It turned to a devil all teeth and claws,
Scratched me and bit me and fled.

To pay for the fish and the milk and the hay
With a purr had been an easy task:
But its hate and my blood were required to pay
For the gifts that it did not ask.

AT THE LAST

Where are you--you whose loving breath
Alone can stay my soul from death?
The world's so wide, I seek it through,
Yet--dare I dream to win to you?
Perhaps your dear desired feet
Pass me in this grey muddy street.
Your face, it may be, has its shrine
In that dull house that's next to mine.
But I believe, O Life, O Fate,
That when I call on Death and wait
One moment at the unclosing gate
I shall turn back for one last gaze
Along the trampled, sordid ways,
And in the sunset see at last,
Just as the barred gate holds me fast,
Your face, your face, too late.

FEAR

If you were here,
Hopes, dreams, ambitions, faith would disappear,
Drowned in your eyes; and I should touch your hand,
Forgetting all that now I understand.

For you confuse my life with memories
Of unrememberable ecstasies
Which were, and are not, and can never be; . . .
Ah! keep the whole earth between you and me.

THE DAY OF JUDGMENT

When the bearing and doing are over,
And no more is to do or bear,
God will see us and judge us
The kind of men we were;
And our sins, so ugly and heavy,
We shall drag them into His sight,
And throw them down at the foot of the throne,
Foul on the steps of light.

We shall not be shamed or frightened,
Though the angels are all at hand,
For He will look at our burden,
And He will understand.
He will turn to the little angels,
Agog to hear and obey,
And point to the festering sin-loads
With, "Take that rubbish away!"

Then the steps will be cleared of the burdens
That we threw down at His feet;
And we shall be washed in the tears of Christ,
And our tears bathe His feet.

And the harvest of all our sinning
That moment's shame will reap -
When we look in the eyes that love us
And know we have made them weep.

A FAREWELL

Good-bye, good-bye; it is not hard to part!
You have my heart--the heart that leaps to hear
Your name called by an echo in a dream;
You have my soul that, like an untroubled stream,
Reflects your soul that leans so dear, so near -
Your heartbeats set the rhythm for my heart.

What more could Life give if we gave her leave
To give, and Life should give us leave to take?
Only each other's arms, each other's eyes,
Each other's lips, the clinging secrecies
That are but as the written words to make
Records of what the heart and soul achieve.

This, only this we yield, my love, my friend,
To Fate's implacable eyes and withering breath.
We still are yours and mine, though, by Time's theft,
My arms are empty and your arms bereft.
It is not hard to part--not harder than Death;
And each of us must face Death in the end!

IN HOSPITAL

Under the shadow of a hawthorn brake,
Where bluebells draw the sky down to the wood,
Where, 'mid brown leaves, the primroses awake
And hidden violets smell of solitude;
Beneath green leaves bright-fluttered by the wing
Of fleeting, beautiful, immortal Spring,
I should have said, "I love you," and your eyes
Have said, "I, too . . . " The gods saw otherwise.

For this is winter, and the London streets
Are full of soldiers from that far, fierce fray
Where life knows death, and where poor glory meets
Full-face with shame, and weeps and turns away.
And in the broken, trampled foreign wood
Is horror, and the terrible scent of blood,
And love shines tremulous, like a drowning star,
Under the shadow of the wings of war.

1916.

PRAYER IN TIME OF WAR

Now Death is near, and very near,
In this wild whirl of horror and fear,
When round the vessel of our State
Roll the great mountain waves of hate.
God! We have but one prayer to-day -
O Father, teach us how to pray.

For prayer is strong, and very strong;
But we have turned from Thee so long
To follow gods that have no power
Save in the safe and sordid hour,
That to Thy feet we have lost the way . . .
O Father, teach us how to pray.

We have done ill, and very ill,
Set up our will against Thy will.
That our soft lives might gorge, full-fed,
We stole our brothers' daily bread.
Lord, we are sorry we went astray -
O Father, teach us how to pray.

Now in this hour of desperate strife
For England's life, her very life,
Teach us to pray that life may be
A new life, beautiful to Thee,
And in Thy hands that life to lay.
O Father, teach us how to pray.

1915.

AT PARTING

Go, since you must, but, Dearest, know
That, Honour having bid you go,
Your honour, if your life be spent,
Shall have a costly monument.

This heart, that fire and roses is
Beneath the magic of your kiss,
Shall turn to marble if you die
And be your deathless effigy.

1914.

INVOCATION

The Spirit of Darkness, the Prince of the Power of the Air,
The terror that walketh by night, and the horror by day,
The legions of Evil, alert and awake and aware,
Press round him each hour; and I pray here alone, far away.

God! call up Thy legions to fight on the side of my love,
Let the seats of the mighty be cast down before him, O Lord,
Send strong wings of angels to shield him beneath and above,
Let glorious Michael unsheath his implacable sword.

Let the whole host of Heaven take part with my dear in his fight,
That the armies of Hell may be scattered like chaff in the blast,
And the trumpets of Heaven blow fair for the triumph of Right.
Inspire him, protect him, and bring him home victor at last.

But if--ah, dear God, give me strength to withhold nothing now! -
If the life of my life be required for Thy splendid design,
Give his country the laurels, though cold and uncrowned be his brow
. . .
Thou gavest Thy Son for the world, and shall I not give mine?

1914.

TO HER: IN TIME OF WAR

Once I made for you songs,
Rondels, triolets, sonnets;
Verse that my love deemed due,
Verse that your love found fair.
Now the wide wings of war
Hang, like a hawk's, over England,
Shadowing meadows and groves;
And the birds and the lovers are mute.

Yet there's a thing to say
Before I go into battle,
Not now a poet's word
But a man's word to his mate:
Dear, if I come back never,

Be it your pride that we gave
The hope of our hearts, each other,
For the sake of the Hope of the World.

1915.

THE FIELDS OF FLANDERS

Last year the fields were all glad and gay
With silver daisies and silver may;
There were kingcups gold by the river's edge
And primrose stars under every hedge.

This year the fields are trampled and brown,
The hedges are broken and beaten down,
And where the primroses used to grow
Are little black crosses set in a row.

And the flower of hopes, and the flowers of dreams,
The noble, fruitful, beautiful schemes,
The tree of life with its fruit and bud,
Are trampled down in the mud and the blood.

The changing seasons will bring again
The magic of Spring to our wood and plain:
Though the Spring be so green as never was seen
The crosses will still be black in the green.

The God of battles shall judge the foe
Who trampled our country and laid her low . . .
God! hold our hands on the reckoning day,
Lest all we owe them we should repay.

1915.

SPRING IN WAR-TIME

Now the sprinkled blackthorn snow
Lies along the lovers' lane
Where last year we used to go -
Where we shall not go again.

In the hedge the buds are new,
By our wood the violets peer -
Just like last year's violets, too,
But they have no scent this year.

Every bird has heart to sing
Of its nest, warmed by its breast;
We had heart to sing last spring,
But we never built our nest.

Presently red roses blown
Will make all the garden gay . . .
Not yet have the daisies grown
On your clay.

1916.

THE MOTHER'S PRAYER

This was my little son
Who leapt and laughed on my knee:
Body we made with love,
Soul made with love by Thee.
This was the mystery
In which I worshipped Thy grace;
This was the sign to me -
The unveiling of Thy face . . .
This, that lies under Thy skies
Naked as on that day
When the floor of heaven gave way
And the glory of God shone through,
When the world was made new
And Thy word was made flesh for me . . .
He lies there, bare to Thy skies,
O Lord God, see!

Body that was in mine
A secret, sacred spell,
Little hands I have kissed
Trampled by beasts in Hell . . .
Growing beauty and grace . . .
Oh, head that lay on my bosom . . .
Broken, battered, shattered . . .
Body that grew like a blossom!
All that was promised me
On my life's royal day.
Every promise broken -

Only a ghost, and clay!

O God, I kneel at Thy feet;
I lay my hands in Thine:
Thou gavest Thy Son for the world,
And shall I not give mine?
Only--O God, have pity!
All my defences are down:
God, I accept the Cross,
Let HIM have the Crown!

By all that my love has borne,
By all that all mothers bear,
By the infinite patient anguish,
By the never-ceasing prayer,
By the thoughts that cut like a living knife,
By the tears that are never dry,
Take what he died to win You -
God, take Your victory!

We have watched on till the light burned low,
And watched the dawn awake;
We have lived hardly and hardly fared
For our sons' sake.
All that was good in Thy earth,
All that taught us of Heaven,
All that we had in the world
We have given.
We pray with empty hands
And hearts that are stiff with pain.
O God! O God! O God!
Let the sacrifice not be vain.
This is his blood, Lord, see!

His blood that was shed for Thee;
Thy banner is dyed in that red tide
Lord, take Thy victory!

God! give Thine angels power
To fight as he fought,
To scatter the hosts of evil,
To bring their boastings to naught -
Gabriel with trumpet of battle . . .
Michael, who wields Thy sword . . .
Breathe Thou Thy spirit upon them,
Put forth Thy strength, O Lord.
See, Lord, this is his body,
Broken for Thee, for Thee . . .
My son, my little son,
Who leapt and laughed on my knee.

"INASMUCH AS YE DID IT NOT . . . "

If Jesus came to London,
Came to London to-day,
He would not go to the West End,
He would come down our way;
He'd talk with the children dancing
To the organ out in the street,
And say he was their big Brother,
And give them something to eat.

He wouldn't go to the mansions
Where the charitable live;
He'd come to the tenement houses
Where we ain't got nothing to give.
He'd come so kind and so homely,
And treat us to beer and bread,
And tell us how we ought to behave;
And we'd try to mind what He said.

In the warm bright West End churches
They sing and preach and pray,
They call us "Beloved brethren,"
But they do not act that way.
And when He came to the church door
He'd call out loud and free,
You stop that preaching and praying
And show what you've done for Me."

Then they'd say, "O Lord, we have given
To the poor both blankets and tracts,
And we've tried to make them sober,
And we've tried to teach them facts.
But they will sneak round to the drink-shop,
And pawn the blankets for beer,
And we find them very ungrateful,
But still we persevere."

Then He would say, "I told you
The time I was here before,
That you were all of you brothers,
All you that I suffered for.
I won't go into your churches,
I'll stop in the sun outside.

You bring out the men your brothers,
The men for whom I died!"

Out of our beastly lodgings,
From arches and doorways about,
They'd have to do as He told them,
They'd have to call us out.
Millions and millions and millions,
Thick and crawling like flies,
We should creep out to the sunshine
And not be afraid of His eyes.

He'd see what God's image looks like
When men have dealt with the same,
Wrinkled with work that is never done,
Swollen and dirty with shame.
He'd see on the children's forehead
The branded gutter-sign
That marks the girls to be harlots,
That dooms the boys to be swine.

Then He'd say, "What's the good of churches
When these have nowhere to sleep?
And how can I hear you praying
When they are cursing so deep?
I gave My Blood and My Body
That they might have bread and wine,
And you have taken your share and theirs
Of these good gifts of mine!"

Then some of the rich would be sorry,
And all would be very scared,
And they'd say, "But we never knew, Lord!"

And He'd say, "You never cared!"
And some would be sick and shameful
Because they'd know that they knew,
And the best would say, "We were wrong, Lord.
Now tell us what to do!"

I think He'd be sitting, likely,
For someone 'ud bring Him a chair,
With a common kid cuddled up on His knee
And the common sun on His hair;
And they'd be standing before Him,
And He'd say, "You know that you knew.
Why haven't you worked for your brothers
The same as I worked for you?

"For since you're all of you brothers
It's clear as God's blessed sun
That each must work for the others,
Not thousands work for one.
And the ones that have lived bone-idle
If they want Me to hear them pray,
Let them go and work for their livings
The only honest way!

"I've got nothing new to tell you,
You know what I always said -
But you've built their bones into churches
And stolen their wine and bread;
You with My Name on your foreheads,
Liar, and traitor, and knave,
You have lived by the death of your brothers,
These whom I died to save!"

I wish He would come and say it;
Perhaps they'd believe it then,
And work like men for their livings
And let us work like men.
Brothers? They don't believe it,
The lie on their lips is red.
They'll never believe till He comes again,
Or till we rise from the dead!

www.bookjungle.com *email: sales@bookjungle.com fax: 630-214-0564 mail: Book Jungle PO Box 2226 Champaign, IL 61825*

The Codes Of Hammurabi And Moses
W. W. Davies

QTY

The discovery of the Hammurabi Code is one of the greatest achievements of archaeology, and is of paramount interest, not only to the student of the Bible, but also to all those interested in ancient history...

Religion   ISBN: *1-59462-338-4*   Pages:132
MSRP $12.95

The Theory of Moral Sentiments
Adam Smith

QTY

This work from 1749. contains original theories of conscience amd moral judgment and it is the foundation for systemof morals.

Philosophy   ISBN: *1-59462-777-0*   Pages:536
MSRP $19.95

Jessica's First Prayer
Hesba Stretton

QTY

In a screened and secluded corner of one of the many railway-bridges which span the streets of London there could be seen a few years ago, from five o'clock every morning until half past eight, a tidily set-out coffee-stall, consisting of a trestle and board, upon which stood two large tin cans, with a small fire of charcoal burning under each so as to keep the coffee boiling during the early hours of the morning when the work-people were thronging into the city on their way to their daily toil...

Childrens   ISBN: *1-59462-373-2*   Pages:84
MSRP $9.95

My Life and Work
Henry Ford

QTY

Henry Ford revolutionized the world with his implementation of mass production for the Model T automobile. Gain valuable business insight into his life and work with his own auto-biography... "We have only started on our development of our country we have not as yet, with all our talk of wonderful progress, done more than scratch the surface. The progress has been wonderful enough but..."

Biographies/   ISBN: *1-59462-198-5*   Pages:300
MSRP $21.95

www.bookjungle.com *email: sales@bookjungle.com fax: 630-214-0564 mail: Book Jungle PO Box 2226 Champaign, IL 61825*

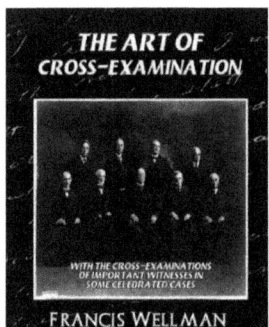

The Art of Cross-Examination
Francis Wellman

QTY

I presume it is the experience of every author, after his first book is published upon an important subject, to be almost overwhelmed with a wealth of ideas and illustrations which could readily have been included in his book, and which to his own mind, at least, seem to make a second edition inevitable. Such certainly was the case with me; and when the first edition had reached its sixth impression in five months, I rejoiced to learn that it seemed to my publishers that the book had met with a sufficiently favorable reception to justify a second and considerably enlarged edition. ..

Reference   ISBN: *1-59462-647-2*   Pages: 412   MSRP *$19.95*

On the Duty of Civil Disobedience
Henry David Thoreau

QTY

Thoreau wrote his famous essay, On the Duty of Civil Disobedience, as a protest against an unjust but popular war and the immoral but popular institution of slave-owning. He did more than write—he declined to pay his taxes, and was hauled off to gaol in consequence. Who can say how much this refusal of his hastened the end of the war and of slavery?

Law   ISBN: *1-59462-747-9*   Pages: 48   MSRP *$7.45*

Dream Psychology Psychoanalysis for Beginners
Sigmund Freud

QTY

Sigmund Freud, born Sigismund Schlomo Freud (May 6, 1856 - September 23, 1939), was a Jewish-Austrian neurologist and psychiatrist who co-founded the psychoanalytic school of psychology. Freud is best known for his theories of the unconscious mind, especially involving the mechanism of repression; his redefinition of sexual desire as mobile and directed towards a wide variety of objects; and his therapeutic techniques, especially his understanding of transference in the therapeutic relationship and the presumed value of dreams as sources of insight into unconscious desires.

Psychology   ISBN: *1-59462-905-6*   Pages: 196   MSRP *$15.45*

The Miracle of Right Thought
Orison Swett Marden

QTY

Believe with all of your heart that you will do what you were made to do. When the mind has once formed the habit of holding cheerful, happy, prosperous pictures, it will not be easy to form the opposite habit. It does not matter how improbable or how far away this realization may see, or how dark the prospects may be, if we visualize them as best we can, as vividly as possible, hold tenaciously to them and vigorously struggle to attain them, they will gradually become actualized, realized in the life. But a desire, a longing without endeavor, a yearning abandoned or held indifferently will vanish without realization.

Self Help   ISBN: *1-59462-644-8*   Pages: 360   MSRP *$25.45*

www.bookjungle.com *email: sales@bookjungle.com fax: 630-214-0564 mail: Book Jungle PO Box 2226 Champaign, IL 61825*

QTY

☐ **The Rosicrucian Cosmo-Conception Mystic Christianity** *by Max Heindel*   ISBN: *1-59462-188-8*   **$38.95**
The Rosicrucian Cosmo-conception is not dogmatic, neither does it appeal to any other authority than the reason of the student. It is: not controversial, but is: sent forth in the, hope that it may help to clear...   New Age/Religion Pages 646

☐ **Abandonment To Divine Providence** *by Jean-Pierre de Caussade*   ISBN: *1-59462-228-0*   **$25.95**
"The Rev. Jean Pierre de Caussade was one of the most remarkable spiritual writers of the Society of Jesus in France in the 18th Century. His death took place at Toulouse in 1751. His works have gone through many editions and have been republished...   Inspirational/Religion Pages 400

☐ **Mental Chemistry** *by Charles Haanel*   ISBN: *1-59462-192-6*   **$23.95**
Mental Chemistry allows the change of material conditions by combining and appropriately utilizing the power of the mind. Much like applied chemistry creates something new and unique out of careful combinations of chemicals the mastery of mental chemistry...   New Age Pages 354

☐ **The Letters of Robert Browning and Elizabeth Barret Barrett 1845-1846 vol II**   ISBN: *1-59462-193-4*   **$35.95**
by Robert Browning and Elizabeth Barrett   Biographies Pages 596

☐ **Gleanings In Genesis (volume I)** *by Arthur W. Pink*   ISBN: *1-59462-130-6*   **$27.45**
Appropriately has Genesis been termed "the seed plot of the Bible" for in it we have, in germ form, almost all of the great doctrines which are afterwards fully developed in the books of Scripture which follow...   Religion/Inspirational Pages 420

☐ **The Master Key** *by L. W. de Laurence*   ISBN: *1-59462-001-6*   **$30.95**
In no branch of human knowledge has there been a more lively increase of the spirit of research during the past few years than in the study of Psychology, Concentration and Mental Discipline. The requests for authentic lessons in Thought Control, Mental Discipline and...   New Age/Business Pages 422

☐ **The Lesser Key Of Solomon Goetia** *by L. W. de Laurence*   ISBN: *1-59462-092-X*   **$9.95**
This translation of the first book of the "Lernegton" which is now for the first time made accessible to students of Talismanic Magic was done, after careful collation and edition, from numerous Ancient Manuscripts in Hebrew, Latin, and French...   New Age/Occult Pages 92

☐ **Rubaiyat Of Omar Khayyam** *by Edward Fitzgerald*   ISBN: *1-59462-332-5*   **$13.95**
Edward Fitzgerald, whom the world has already learned, in spite of his own efforts to remain within the shadow of anonymity, to look upon as one of the rarest poets of the century, was born at Bredfield, in Suffolk, on the 31st of March, 1809. He was the third son of John Purcell...   Music Pages 172

☐ **Ancient Law** *by Henry Maine*   ISBN: *1-59462-128-4*   **$29.95**
The chief object of the following pages is to indicate some of the earliest ideas of mankind, as they are reflected in Ancient Law, and to point out the relation of those ideas to modern thought.   Religion/History Pages 452

☐ **Far-Away Stories** *by William J. Locke*   ISBN: *1-59462-129-2*   **$19.45**
"Good wine needs no bush, but a collection of mixed vintages does. And this book is just such a collection. Some of the stories I do not want to remain buried for ever in the museum files of dead magazine-numbers an author's not unpardonable vanity..."   Fiction Pages 272

☐ **Life of David Crockett** *by David Crockett*   ISBN: *1-59462-250-7*   **$27.45**
"Colonel David Crockett was one of the most remarkable men of the times in which he lived. Born in humble life, but gifted with a strong will, an indomitable courage, and unremitting perseverance...   Biographies/New Age Pages 424

☐ **Lip-Reading** *by Edward Nitchie*   ISBN: *1-59462-206-X*   **$25.95**
Edward B. Nitchie, founder of the New York School for the Hard of Hearing, now the Nitchie School of Lip-Reading, Inc, wrote "LIP-READING Principles and Practice". The development and perfecting of this meritorious work on lip-reading was an undertaking...   How-to Pages 400

☐ **A Handbook of Suggestive Therapeutics, Applied Hypnotism, Psychic Science**   ISBN: *1-59462-214-0*   **$24.95**
by Henry Munro   Health/New Age/Health/Self-help Pages 376

☐ **A Doll's House: and Two Other Plays** *by Henrik Ibsen*   ISBN: *1-59462-112-8*   **$19.95**
Henrik Ibsen created this classic when in revolutionary 1848 Rome. Introducing some striking concepts in playwriting for the realist genre, this play has been studied the world over.   Fiction/Classics/Plays 308

☐ **The Light of Asia** *by sir Edwin Arnold*   ISBN: *1-59462-204-3*   **$13.95**
In this poetic masterpiece, Edwin Arnold describes the life and teachings of Buddha. The man who was to become known as Buddha to the world was born as Prince Gautama of India but he rejected the worldly riches and abandoned the reigns of power when...   Religion/History/Biographies Pages 170

☐ **The Complete Works of Guy de Maupassant** *by Guy de Maupassant*   ISBN: *1-59462-157-8*   **$16.95**
"For days and days, nights and nights, I had dreamed of that first kiss which was to consecrate our engagement, and I knew not on what spot I should put my lips..."   Fiction/Classics Pages 240

☐ **The Art of Cross-Examination** *by Francis L. Wellman*   ISBN: *1-59462-309-0*   **$26.95**
Written by a renowned trial lawyer, Wellman imparts his experience and uses case studies to explain how to use psychology to extract desired information through questioning.   How-to/Science/Reference Pages 408

☐ **Answered or Unanswered?** *by Louisa Vaughan*   ISBN: *1-59462-248-5*   **$10.95**
Miracles of Faith in China   Religion Pages 112

☐ **The Edinburgh Lectures on Mental Science (1909)** *by Thomas*   ISBN: *1-59462-008-3*   **$11.95**
This book contains the substance of a course of lectures recently given by the writer in the Queen Street Hall, Edinburgh. Its purpose is to indicate the Natural Principles governing the relation between Mental Action and Material Conditions...   New Age/Psychology Pages 148

☐ **Ayesha** *by H. Rider Haggard*   ISBN: *1-59462-301-5*   **$24.95**
Verily and indeed it is the unexpected that happens! Probably if there was one person upon the earth from whom the Editor of this, and of a certain previous history, did not expect to hear again...   Classics Pages 380

☐ **Ayala's Angel** *by Anthony Trollope*   ISBN: *1-59462-352-X*   **$29.95**
The two girls were both pretty, but Lucy who was twenty-one who supposed to be simple and comparatively unattractive, whereas Ayala was credited, as her Bombwhat romantic name might show, with poetic charm and a taste for romance. Ayala when her father died was nineteen...   Fiction Pages 484

☐ **The American Commonwealth** *by James Bryce*   ISBN: *1-59462-286-8*   **$34.45**
An interpretation of American democratic political theory. It examines political mechanics and society from the perspective of Scotsman James Bryce   Politics Pages 572

☐ **Stories of the Pilgrims** *by Margaret P. Pumphrey*   ISBN: *1-59462-116-0*   **$17.95**
This book explores pilgrims religious oppression in England as well as their escape to Holland and eventual crossing to America on the Mayflower, and their early days in New England...   History Pages 268

www.bookjungle.com email: sales@bookjungle.com fax: 630-214-0564 mail: Book Jungle PO Box 2226 Champaign, IL 61825

QTY

The Fasting Cure *by Sinclair Upton* ISBN: *1-59462-222-1* **$13.95**
In the Cosmopolitan Magazine for May, 1910, and in the Contemporary Review (London) for April, 1910, I published an article dealing with my experiences in fasting. I have written a great many magazine articles, but never one which attracted so much attention... *New Age/Self Help/Health Pages 164*

Hebrew Astrology *by Sepharial* ISBN: *1-59462-308-2* **$13.45**
In these days of advanced thinking it is a matter of common observation that we have left many of the old landmarks behind and that we are now pressing forward to greater heights and to a wider horizon than that which represented the mind-content of our progenitors... *Astrology Pages 144*

Thought Vibration or The Law of Attraction in the Thought World ISBN: *1-59462-127-6* **$12.95**
by William Walker Atkinson *Psychology/Religion Pages 144*

Optimism *by Helen Keller* ISBN: *1-59462-108-X* **$15.95**
Helen Keller was blind, deaf, and mute since 19 months old, yet famously learned how to overcome these handicaps, communicate with the world, and spread her lectures promoting optimism. An inspiring read for everyone... *Biographies/Inspirational Pages 84*

Sara Crewe *by Frances Burnett* ISBN: *1-59462-360-0* **$9.45**
In the first place, Miss Minchin lived in London. Her home was a large, dull, tall one, in a large, dull square, where all the houses were alike, and all the sparrows were alike, and where all the door-knockers made the same heavy sound... *Childrens/Classic Pages 88*

The Autobiography of Benjamin Franklin *by Benjamin Franklin* ISBN: *1-59462-135-7* **$24.95**
The Autobiography of Benjamin Franklin has probably been more extensively read than any other American historical work, and no other book of its kind has had such ups and downs of fortune. Franklin lived for many years in England, where he was agent... *Biographies/History Pages 332*

Name	
Email	
Telephone	
Address	
City, State ZIP	

☐ Credit Card   ☐ Check / Money Order

Credit Card Number	
Expiration Date	
Signature	

Please Mail to: Book Jungle
PO Box 2226
Champaign, IL 61825
or Fax to: 630-214-0564

ORDERING INFORMATION
web: *www.bookjungle.com*
email: *sales@bookjungle.com*
fax: *630-214-0564*
mail: *Book Jungle PO Box 2226 Champaign, IL 61825*
or PayPal *to sales@bookjungle.com*

Please contact us for bulk discounts

DIRECT-ORDER TERMS

20% Discount if You Order Two or More Books
Free Domestic Shipping!
Accepted: Master Card, Visa, Discover, American Express

www.ingramcontent.com/pod-product-compliance
Lightning Source LLC
Chambersburg PA
CBHW081325040426
42453CB00013B/2305